The Dying Gaul

The Dying Gaul

by

Craig Lucas

STAGE & SCREEN

The Book Club for the Performing Arts

Author's Preface

The Dying Gaul was written in twelve days in the summer of 1996. My boyfriend, Patrick William Barnes, suffered through every minute of it and subsequent assaults the play received through a year of constructive criticism. I thank him. I also wish to thank by name the extraordinary array of artists and friends and artist-friends who helped me steer the play out of its hiding place: Mark Brokaw, Doug Aibel, Linda Emond, Tim Hopper, Cotter Smith, Tony Goldwyn, Robert Emmett Lunney, Jerry Patch, Deborah Eisenberg, Wallace Shawn, André Bishop, Peter Manning, Michael Wilson, Joe Mantello, Tony Kushner, Rosalyn Elisabeth Coleman, David Stone, Susan Gallin, Michael John La Chiusa, and Diana Carulli. Lastly I extend my thanks to Mark Lamos, Greg Leaming and the Hartford Stage Co. for commissioning the play.

Now some people, albeit a minority, encountered the play for the first time and liked it *up to the point it turned violent*. (This may have included the *Times* critic who seems like a very nice man who much prefers my play *Prelude To A Kiss*. I agree, it's a lovely play. I hope we'll see a lot of it in years to come, and also that its virtues won't prevent me from writing other, perhaps even *different* plays as time goes on.) These people felt the play's resolution was unearned. It was "too surprising." This resolution implies condemnation of the choices made by the play's central character, a seemingly-lovely gay man who had never hurt anyone before, who was in fact a "victim" of terrible loss. Whatever its intrinsic value, this criticism of the play's conclusion also speaks volumes about those leveling it. Where did so many of us learn to believe that the victims of terrible loss are ennobled by their suffering? Though I'm sure some people are ennobled, me, I've come out of the experience rather the worse for wear.

My lover, my best friend, my closest colleague over decades, my mother, my father-in-law, and another several dozen friends, ex-lovers and colleagues all died rather horrible deaths in rather rapid succession, and I did not find myself ascending into a compassionate, giving place, but rather a significantly meaner and less generous one. And this play is the best that I could make of my newfound insights into the nature of the beast. The human one. Aristotle thought it was edifying to watch terrible things happen to noble people. Why this should be so, I do not know. But you've got to hand it to him for noticing the phenomenon.

The Greek concept of *Ate* is one that few people seem to remark on anymore, but which is entirely familiar to anyone who has suffered grievously, or celebrated their own boundless desires. Or both. This is a play about *Ate*, at least in so far as I view it. Every single day the TV and newspapers and movies tell us there will be no cost for our myriad purchases.

I don't agree.

—CRAIG LUCAS
November 1998

Craig Lucas' THE DYING GAUL premiered at the Vineyard Theatre on September 18, 1998. It was directed by Mark Brokaw. The scenic design was by Allen Moyer, costume design was by Jess Goldstein, the lighting design was by Christopher Ackerlind and the original music and sound design was by David Van Tieghem. The production stage manager was Amy Patricia Stern. Casting was by Janet Foster. Press representative was Shirley Herz Associates.

THE CAST

(In Order of Appearance)

Robert	TIM HOPPER
Jeffrey	COTTER SMITH
Elaine	LINDA EDMOND
Foss	ROBERT EMMET LUNNEY

The Dying Gaul takes place in 1995 in Los Angeles, California

"Woe to him who seeks to please rather than to appall."

Herman Melville, *Moby Dick*

For Tony Kushner

ACT I

ACT I

ACT I

Robert alone.

Robert: "Self-salvation is for any man the immediate task. If a man lay wounded by a poisoned arrow he would not delay extraction by demanding details of the man who shot it, or the length and make of the arrow. Begin now by facing life as it is, learning always by direct and personal experience."

(Jeffrey's office. Jeffrey and Robert)

Jeffrey: So, Robert . . . do people call you Robert or Bob?

Robert: Both.

Jeffrey: Which do you prefer?

Robert: I don't . . . I sort of like to see which they prefer and then that tells them something, tells me something about them.

Jeffrey: I gotcha. Interesting. You're a very good writer.

Robert: Thank you.

(Pause)

Jeffrey: What kind of movies do you like? You like movies?

Robert: Oh yeah.

Jeffrey: You do. What are some of your favorite movies?

Robert: Oh, you know, I like all kinds of movies.

Jeffrey: You do.

Robert: Oh yeah, I like, you know, movie movies, and I like old movies and foreign movies.

(*Pause*)

Jeffrey: What was your favorite movie last year?

Robert: Last year? I don't really go in for favorites, you know, I sort of think each movie, like each painting or book or . . . national park . . . is actually unique and to be appreciated as such, god I sound like an English professor, I like . . . I liked very much . . . um . . . I thought that, uh . . .

Jeffrey: That's okay.

Robert: No, I liked that English—*Remains of the Day*, and I loved the dinosaur movie. I mean I like all uh . . . every thing along the continuum.

(*Short pause*)

Jeffrey: Well, we're interested in your script.

Robert: What?

Jeffrey: We're interested in *The Dying Gaul*.

(*Short pause*)

Robert: Okay.

Jeffrey: So. That's that . . .

(*Short pause*)

Your agent is . . . ?

Robert: Dead.

Jeffrey: Oh.

Robert: Yeah. Malcolm Cartonis.

Jeffrey: I'm sorry.

(*Pause*)

Robert: Yeah.

Jeffrey: Who's . . . taken over for him?

Robert: Well, nobody, unfortunately, he was kind of a one-man band . . .

Jeffrey: Well, a good one, obviously, because he got us the script and I read it and Kohlberg's read it.

Robert: He has?

Jeffrey: Yes. We don't greenlight anything without his approval.

Robert: Greenlight?

Jeffrey: No, I'm not saying we're making your script, I'm saying we've all read it and we all think it's good . . . and that's why I'm talking to you. (*Intercom buzzes*) Yes?

Woman's Voice: Your wife.

Jeffrey: All right. (*To Robert*) Excuse me. (*Into receiver*) Hi . . . Sure . . . Sure . . . Sure . . . Sure . . . Okay. Love you too. (*He hangs up*) Where do you think you want to go with the script?

Robert: I'm sorry?

5

Jeffrey: Where else do you want to go with the script?

Robert: Well, I . . . I guess I could take it to some of the independents.

Jeffrey: No, no, no . . . what a doll you are. What kind of work do you want to do on it?

Robert: Oh. Oh, sorry . . .

Jeffrey: That's okay. That was just so sweet. From acceptance to total rejection, you took it all in stride. What kinds of things have you thought about, or do you think it's finished as it is?

Robert: Well, it's as far as I could take it without some sort of input from a director.

Jeffrey: Uh-huh. And who's your dream director?

Robert: Oh, Gus Van Sant, I guess. Since Truffaut's dead.

Jeffrey: Good. He's very good. Would you like me to show him the script?

Robert: Yeah, sure, why not?

Jeffrey: Good. 'Cause I already have. And he likes it.

Robert: Do you have any smelling salts?

Jeffrey: You're really very charming. He likes it very much, and he has some questions as we all do, and . . . who knows if he's the right person or not, but I wanted to talk to you first before we set up a meeting. What's the title, explain the title to me.

Robert: Well, you know, they go to that museum in Rome . . .

Jeffrey: Ken and Maurice.

Robert: . . . and they see the sculpture . . .

Jeffrey: Yeah, yeah, yeah, but why is that the name of the movie?

Robert: Because. Oh, I see, because they feel that the statue depicting the, like, the defeated, the vanquished . . .

Jeffrey: Uh-huh.

Robert: . . . and dying soldier, and the Gauls fought naked and without armor . . .

Jeffrey: Right.

Robert: —so he's so young and defenseless . . .

Jeffrey: Beautiful.

Robert: With just this little hole in his side . . . otherwise . . . and being that the statue is *by* a Roman, by one of those whose side was responsible for all the slaughter, it would be like an American making a statue honoring the suffering of . . . one of the countries we've fought, a person from . . .

Jeffrey: From where?

Robert: One of, whatever countries we've invaded, not invaded. You know what I'm saying. Like . . .

Jeffrey: Okay, so, Ken and Maurice see this sculpture of this . . . Gaul. Who is dying . . . and?

Robert: And they identify with the Gaul in a way because they're gay and so many of their friends are dying and they keep looking for some kind of response from the enemy . . .

Jeffrey: Right?

Robert: And then remember where they talk about the sculpture and say, "Well, what good did it do the poor guy who bled to death, the guy in the—?"

Jeffrey: Right. Right.

Robert: But at least . . . maybe . . . some kind of compassion was awakened in the Romans, and maybe at some time in the future as a result of someone *seeing* the sculpture, maybe some other . . .

Jeffrey: Gaul.

Robert: . . . was, somebody took pity or spared some other French peasant from . . .

Jeffrey: Yeah, I get it. That's very . . .

Robert: It's kind of oblique.

Jeffrey: No, I understand, and it has a political overtone.

Robert: That's right. Which I imagine . . .

Jeffrey: No, no, we're not afraid of that, we're not afraid of anything, the idea, obviously, is to reach as many people as possible and to have the broadest appeal, so that we can make money, but also so that . . . to whatever degree the movie affects people, it can also serve as a kind of Dying Gaul for the viewers. I mean, if you even look at a movie like . . . well, say, just to pick something, *Tootsie*, which we didn't make but which is a very good movie—

Robert: It's a great comedy.

Jeffrey: It says something . . . in a small, but totally amusing way . . . and you don't see it coming: about men and women. The guy is an arrogant . . . you know, chauvinist, and he, for his own reasons, dresses up, feels he has to dress up as a woman, and as a result, he learns something about what it means to be a man. He finds, it's so obvious, if you know it's there, but he finds a feminine side to himself and vows, you don't actually see it happen, but you know he does it—

Robert: Uh-huh.

Jeffrey: —he vows not to be such an asshole, and you feel good for him.

Robert: Yeah.

Jeffrey: So that's the kind of political statement you can slip an audience without their feeling they've been had or they're being lectured.

Robert: Right.

Jeffrey: And . . . well, *The Dying Gaul* isn't a comedy, it's a weepie, what I call—like *Terms of Endearment*. And these movies are *Very. Hard. To sell.*

(*Pause*)

Robert: Uh-huh.

Jeffrey: They're *Very. Hard.*

(*Pause*)

Jeffrey: And they're my favorite kind of movie. They just have to be made with care. And . . . *The Silence of the Lambs* is another one which touches on feminist ideology without. . . . Did you like that movie?

Robert: Yes and no.

(*Short pause*)

Jeffrey: Okay.

Robert: Did you make it?

Jeffrey: No, no. No, no. . . . Why didn't you like it?

Robert: The, uh, faggy portrayal of the killer.

Jeffrey: He's not gay. Jamie Gumm is not gay.

Robert: Yeah, that's what I heard, but I think that's a bunch of bullshit. Because he has the poodle—

Jeffrey: I had a poodle. My wife and I had a poodle.

Robert: Yeah, but I bet you don't wear nipple rings and put on eyeliner and, you probably don't cut up women because you want to be one.

(*Pause*)

Jeffrey: You never know.

Robert: True.

(*Short pause*)

Jeffrey: So what are we gonna do? Do you want to sell this script?

Robert: Sure.

Jeffrey: And . . . do you want to do the re-writes?

Robert: Well . . . what do you mean?

Jeffrey: I mean . . . are you interested in doing the re-writes or do you want to sell the script outright?

Robert: I don't ... *of course*. I don't want somebody else ...

Jeffrey: Okay.

Robert: ... mucking around with this—

Jeffrey: Good. Great. I'm glad you're ... I'm sorry you don't have an agent, though. Are you going to sign with somebody else?

Robert: Oh, I don't know, Malcolm was a really close friend and ... (*Short pause*) I haven't been able to find another agent.

(*Pause*)

Jeffrey: We can deal directly with you. Or recommend a lawyer. Oh, I should let business affairs call you, we should stick to the artistic discussion. They'll offer you more than minimum, so, with the re-writes, you know, this could be a couple hundred thousand, but ... don't let that sway you. What? Okay, so ... I understand your reasons for wanting the men to be men, because of the political dimension, but ... Ken and Maurice.

Robert: I'm not making them heterosexual.

Jeffrey: No, no. *Please.*

Robert: I'm sorry.

Jeffrey: No, I mean, I understand ... I read your script, Robert, I know what kind of person you are.

Robert: I'm sorry.

Jeffrey: I'm not asking you to jettison any of your principles.

11

(*Pause*)

Robert: Sorry.

Jeffrey: We like. Your script. (*Intercom buzzes*) Hold all my calls. (*Silence*) What . . . Presumably you are looking for something universal . . . in the experience of two gay men . . . which a wider audience can identify with.

Robert: You could say that.

Jeffrey: Would that be a true statement? Okay. You want to reach as many people as possible with the universal human . . . *truth* about these two characters. One of whom is a Person With AIDS. Now. Don't. Say. Anything . . . until . . . okay. Most Americans. Hate. Gay people. They hear it's about gay people, they won't go.

Robert: What about *Philadelphia*?

Jeffrey: *Philadelphia* is about a man who hates gay people. Period. And it's been done. To get people into the theater, the movie theater, they have to think it's going to be fun. Or sensational. Or . . . some kind of—make them feel fantastic about themselves. No one. Goes to the movies. To have a bad time. Or to learn anything. To be improved. Do we agree with this?

(*Pause*)

Robert: Yes.

Jeffrey: What is important is what they leave the theater with. Yes? . . . And if they don't . . . *enterrrrrr* . . . the theater, they don't get a chance to leave it. Is this all acceptable to you . . . as a thesis?

(*Pause*)

12

Jeffrey: No one is going to see *The Dying Gaul*. If you make it with Tom Cruise—who wouldn't go near it for a hundred million dollars, oh fuck, he'd blow me and you for a hundred million dollars, but you know what I'm saying, and with . . . Clint Eastwood . . . and got Steven Spielberg to direct it and released it in two hundred million screens . . . no one. Is going. To see. *The Dying. Gaul. (Pause)* I am sorry. Now. If we make Maurice a woman dying of AIDS, and let's face it, heterosexuals are also getting AIDS, in disastrous numbers.

Robert: I want nothing to do with this.

Jeffrey: We'll write our own script based loosely on *The Dying Gaul*—

Robert: Fine.

Jeffrey: Or we'll give you one million dollars for your script.

(Pause)

Robert: A million dollars?

Jeffrey: With which you can go out and write four hundred new screenplays about men with, gay men with AIDS, without AIDS, a gay love story, whatever is the most important to you.

Robert: If you want the script so much—

Jeffrey: We think it is good. We want to make your script, and we will pay you for it. We will not make *The Dying Gaul* with two men in bed, falling in love, surviving pain and all the blah blah blah, it's not going to happen. Ever. Ever. Ever. I will guarantee you the first re-write, *twice* scale, because you are a wonderful writer, with a beautiful visual sense, and a realistic understanding of forward action, which is not nothing, and an appreciation of the innate laws of storytelling as it directly relates to movie-making, and there are about mmmmmaybe twenty of you. In the world. We want your script. We want you to re-write it.

Robert: This is so . . .

Jeffrey: I know. Sit down. (*Pause*) Please? You don't have to stay, or agree, you just, you could listen.

Robert: Ohhh . . .

(*Pause*)

Jeffrey: There can be minor characters who are gay. They don't have to be gags.

Robert: Oh, they can be noble, right?

Jeffrey: They don't have to be noble. They can be whatever you want. They cannot be the center of the story, because the center of the country is not gay and the center of the country is what pays for the movies to be made.

Robert: The center of the country isn't black, either, but they made *Malcolm X*.

Jeffrey: Yes. In fifty or twenty-five or maybe even who knows how many years we can make the gay version of *Malcolm X*, and people will go, but they will not go now in 1995, and how we know this is empirical observation.

(*Pause*)

Robert: Were you serious about the million dollars?

Jeffrey: Are we having a conversation, Robert—

Robert: I'm going to take the script to Paramount—

Jeffrey: Yes, we are serious about the million dollars.

Robert: Somebody wants to be in my movie. Who wants to be in my movie?

Jeffrey: I told you that Gus Van Sant is interested, he has not committed—

Robert: Oh come on, you're not gonna let Gus Van Sant direct this movie until he makes a giant blockbuster which he will never do—

Jeffrey: He might.

Robert: —and you'll fire him before we ever go into production and bring in Joel Fucking Schumacher.

Jeffrey: It's not a bad idea, you know, and he's gay!

Robert: *Who wants to be in the movie?* Tell me now or it's a million and a half.

Jeffrey: Tom Cruise and Michelle Pfeiffer. And Denzel Washington, Martin Sheen, Jim Carrey and Winona Rider, Meg Ryan, Daniel Day Lewis, Debra Winger and Johnny Depp . . . among others. I wish you would sit.

Robert: Word travels fast. Who wants to play Maurice?

Jeffrey: They all want to play Maurice, but we can work that out.

(*Pause*)

Robert: You have virtually no idea how much one million dollars would mean in my life. I live in a basement apartment that floods when it rains, because I am still paying off my college loan. I have a son for whom I pay child support, and Malcolm who just died, my agent, was also my lover.

(*Pause*)

Jeffrey: I'm sorry.

Robert: I can't in good conscience . . . take this money from you.

Jeffrey: You are an amazing and lovely person, Robert, and you have succeeded in making me feel like a total scumbag.

Robert: Good. I'm glad.

(*Pause*)

Jeffrey: How's your health?

Robert: It's okay. I'm negative.

Jeffrey: Good.

Robert: Yeah, I check it every two seconds, Maurice and—I mean Malcolm, god oh god, Malcolm and I always had safe sex. Can't I write you a new script, something altogether—

Jeffrey: We want *The Dying Gaul*, and we want you to write it. Take the million and write something else.

(*Pause*)

Robert: Oh Jesus . . .

Jeffrey: Yes? (*Pause. Robert nods. Into the intercom*) Liz, would you call Albert in Business Affairs and ask him to come on down here, please, give me two minutes. (*Pause*) Congratulations. You are a millionaire. (*Pause*) Do you want to see the brand new Mike Leigh? Have you seen it?

Robert: No.

Jeffrey: Are you interested?

Robert: Sure.

Jeffrey (*into the intercom*): Liz, would you arrange a private screening for this evening with Robert Isaacson and me for the Mike Leigh, then book a table at Spago for ten-thirty—(*To Robert*) You have plans?

Robert: No. No.

Jeffrey (*into intercom*): And call my wife and tell her I have to work late, please, tell her I'll call her from the restaurant. (*Pause*) You're very talented, and very lucky, and so are we. I feel good about this, Robert . . . I want you to feel good. (*Short pause*) Yes? (*Pause*) What's wrong?

Robert: I can't really . . . I can't say.

Jeffrey: What? Tell me? (*Short pause*) Hey. Hey. Hey. Hey. It's going to be a beautiful movie, and you are going to write more movies, and some day . . . you are going to be able to write your own. Ticket. Do you . . . Look at me. I mean that . . . I mean that, Robert. Look at Spike Lee. He makes movies he cares about. . . . About his own people. And they make money. And that will happen. For you. I want that for you. Come here . . . Give me a hug. (*They hug*) Okay? (*Robert nods*) You are very very handsome . . . And I'm getting . . . a little . . . turned on . . . Are you? (*Short pause*) You can do anything you want. As long as you don't call it what it is. You understand?

———

(*Robert alone*)

Robert: "The first fact of existence is the law of change or impermanence. Life is a bridge, therefore build no house on it. Whosoever clings to any form, however splendid, will suffer by resisting the flow."

———————

(*Jeffrey's home. Robert, Elaine, and Jeffrey*)

Robert: So beautiful.

Elaine: Well, spend a few hours driving around up here in the canyon and nearby, you'll sneer at us.

(*Short pause*)

Robert: But your garden.

Jeffrey: Two seconds, sorry!

Robert: These incredible bromeliads.

Elaine: You know plants?

Robert: Some. Malcolm, my lover who . . .

Elaine: Yes.

Robert: Was obsessed with herbs and all flowers, he knew everything.

Elaine: You have a garden?

Robert: Well, I have the remnants of what he left in a, oh, it's a little fenced in plot behind my apartment; when he was really sick, I, he would tell me what to pull up, when to water . . . Now it's . . .

Elaine: I don't have a single idea what all this is, the gardener put everything in, I planted these couple of lettuces and mache or these edible flowers—

Robert: Nasturtium.

Elaine: —in between, so I could make fresh salads which I hardly ever do.

Robert: You should, I think you should be careful about—

Jeffrey (*overlapping to Elaine*): Offer him something to drink.

Robert: I think this here might be monkshood—

Jeffrey: Baby?

Elaine: What can I get you to drink?

Robert: Oh, gosh, I feel I should say spring water, but I'd really like a vodka.

Elaine: Peppered? Lemon? Ketel One?

Robert: Oh, I'll drink 'em all and we'll stay all night. Just a plain . . . But you know—

Elaine (*overlapping*): Up?

Robert: Sure. But . . . you should . . . (*Elaine exits*) Some of these . . .

(*Jeffrey is on hold*)

Jeffrey: Some view, huh?

Robert: Oh god.

Jeffrey: There are days I can't believe, I wake up early or come home especially late— (*Into the phone*) Uh-huh? Okay. (*He hangs up*) I'll look out and think: I live here. This is actually my home. When is someone going to march in and demand the keys back . . .

(He kisses Robert, gropes him)

Robert: Should . . . ?

Jeffrey: It's okay. I want to suck you until there isn't a drop of juice left and then lick you from head to toe . . . and . . . and have you inside— *(Elaine returns)* —the foreign markets and video, you'll be able to have a second house looking down on *us* . . .

Elaine: Oh, everyone looks down on us, that's nothing. What part of town do you live in, Robert?

Robert: Oh god. I live in West Hollywood in a rental.

Jeffrey: Not for long.

Robert: Oh, I don't want to change anything, not for now. I don't want to get used to . . .

Elaine: Oh, you will. Elevator going up! Up and up; the context shifts, things you thought were luxuries become essential . . .

Robert: Uh-huh.

Elaine: Suddenly your decisions are . . . *informed* by your desire to own *another* Balthus.

Jeffrey: Darling. He's just made the first money he's ever seen in his life, he's paying child support and alimony, he's not thinking about . . .

Elaine: No? Take a look at *Faust*, that's all I'm saying. Decide for yourself.

Jeffrey: They told me not to marry Cassandra, but I don't know, she seemed so . . . prescient.

(*Pause*)

Elaine: How many kids do you have?

Robert: One. We had him the second it was clear to both of us that our love was probably not gonna make me straight, and I think we thought in that . . . idiotic way of our . . . fear and twenty-four-ish-ness . . . that . . .

Elaine: Oh, but you must love him.

Robert: Oh yeah, but . . . Yeah, of course. He's . . . he's my life now. He and his mom live in New York.

(*Pause*)

Elaine: I'm sorry about your friend. (*Short pause*) When did he die?

Robert: January.

Elaine: Of this year?

Robert: Uh-huh.

Elaine: So you're still . . .

Robert: Uh-huh.

Elaine: Oh god.

Jeffrey: . . . Rough.

(*Pause*)

Robert: Sides of me . . . things I didn't know were there have sprung up . . . taken over.

Elaine: Such as?

Robert: Oh, I'm like famished, you know, for distraction.

Elaine: Such—

Jeffrey: Well, I mean, that—it stands to reason.

Robert: Oh . . . the computer.

Elaine: I just got my first.

Robert: Oh really?

Jeffrey: As we limp into modernity . . . the last on the block to have e-mail at home.

Elaine: I hear it's already passé, I'm so . . .

Robert: Oh, not to me. Send me e-mail, I'll answer, I sit all day, days in a row—surfing the Internet!

Elaine: Do you do those chat rooms? (*To Jeffrey*) What? He doesn't have to answer.

Robert: No, I don't mind. I love them. Actually. They're like life after death, I think . . .

Elaine: How so?

Robert: There's all these voices, you know? (*Jeffrey's cell phone rings*) . . . these disembodied . . . souls . . .

Jeffrey (*into phone*): Yeah . . . Oh, fuck him . . . *Fuck* him . . . No, tell him I said it . . . I'm perfectly—This is, okay—

Elaine: Go on. Please.

Robert: No faces, no cor—

Jeffrey (*same time*): This is my message: Fuck you, Scott. Fuck—If he asks—

Elaine: Jeff!

Jeffrey: —why I'm angry, tell him I said "Fuck. You."

(*Jeffrey's conversation continues, unheard*)

Robert: Sorry. No corporeal being at all—

Elaine: Uh-huh.

Robert: . . . floating in this . . . *place* where, that doesn't even exist, really . . . You . . . only touch in the sense that you see a reflection of them and they see some sort of reflection of you, but only what you want them to see: it can be the most essential part of you, but that's your choice, you know?

Elaine: Well . . . not really; I haven't seen them, I've only heard.

Robert: I mean, well, the Buddhists—You know anything about Buddhism?—Buddhists believe that the only thing after life is the cumulative effect of our actions: karma, and that's what it's like, all this karma just colliding in the middle of *nowhere*—

(*Jeffrey hangs up and re-emerges*)

Elaine: Uh-huh. But I'm interested in hearing about the sex part.

Jeffrey: Of course you are, and that's why we love you, more vodka, Robert?

Robert: No. Yes, please.

Elaine: You want to, hey, you want to see my . . . *llllaptop?*

Robert: Sssssssure.

Jeffrey (*overlapping*): Oh, great.

(*Jeffrey exists. Elaine gets her laptop*)

Elaine: I can't figure out a fucking thing about this thing . . . Jeffrey's busy making his . . . twelve figures and my kids are too young . . . The guy—

Robert: Oh, wow, look at this.

Elaine: Is it good?

Robert: Well, it's kind of a Silver Cloud compared to my used bicycle.

(*Jeffrey returns with bottle of vodka*)

Jeffrey: Let me just say that we have to be relatively sober, or I do, by the time the scores come in after the screening . . .

Elaine: I hate hate hate hate these screenings.

Jeffrey: You don't have to go.

Elaine: I hear about a project for years sometimes and never meet the writers until we go to the mall. I think they should spell it M-A-U-L. So I insisted on meeting you before I had to see you completely crestfallen—whenever your movie does get made—shaken, trembling, cast aside. And Jeffrey made you sound like there was a glint of a human being in there, so I had to see for myself. Watch everyone's faces when the scores come in. Just *watch*.

Jeffrey: It isn't—

Elaine: The harder the writers have struggled to keep some sort of sense or artistry or meaning in their story—

Jeffrey: It—

Elaine: —the worse the picture does, always, because Jeffrey is always right . . . (*To Jeffrey*) Hm?

Jeffrey: Nothing.

Elaine: Maybe as a Buddhist you won't be so susceptible to all that.

Jeffrey: You're a Buddhist?

Robert: Well . . .

Elaine: So show me how to get online. Oh, I'm already on. *Rob131*?

Robert: I signed on as your guest.

Elaine: So this is the name you use . . . ?

Robert: Sometimes. You can have as many names as you want.

Elaine: You can?

Robert: Make up a completely different profile.

Elaine: So for every facet of your personality . . . ?

Robert: Exactly.

Elaine: Mmm. So how do we get to the really filthy rooms?

Jeffrey: Yeah, I want to see, too.

Elaine: I can sign on, and that's about it.

Robert: Okay, let's see, click on MEMBER rooms—

Elaine: And then you see peoples' members?

Robert: Well, you can, actually, I mean, you know, people send naked photos . . . Here, I like this room, *Men-4MenParkBench*.

Elaine: Park bench?

Robert: Yeah, you know, you pretend you're sitting on or sometimes under or maybe, you know, walking by a park bench and then . . . stuff happens . . .

Elaine: How?

Robert: What do you mean?

Elaine: What happens?

Jeffrey: Nothing, that's the point: safe sex.

Elaine: But, okay, can I just ask how you type and do that at the same time?

Robert: Well, you alternate.

Jeffrey: Isn't this nice we're all getting to know one another so fast?

Robert: So you can click on someone's name—

Elaine: *ILove2Lick*!?

Robert: —and check their profile.

Jeffrey: We gotta go, kids.

Elaine: "Investment banker. Affectionate, tactile, roMAN-tic—"

Jeffrey: Gotta go.

Elaine: "Discrete, no guy can be too hairy—"

Jeffrey: I agree, but we can just make it in time if we—

Elaine (*overlapping*): "My idea of a quickie is the entire weekend—"

Jeffrey (*continuous*): —leave now—

Elaine: "Let me teach you the Vulcan Lip Lock!" No wonder you—

Jeffrey: All aboard that's going ashore!

Elaine (*without stopping*): —want to do this all the time—

Jeffrey: Elaine—!

Elaine (*overlapping, exiting*): I gotta pee, you're the boss, Jeff, Jesus, you've kept me waiting often enough!

(*She is gone*)

Jeffrey: She insisted. She had to meet you. Least this way she won't suspect.

Robert (*mouthed*): SH!

Jeffrey: No, we had cork put in every room so we could be as loud as we liked, Max and Debbon couldn't hear us when we came. FUCK ME, ROBERT, COME ON! INSIDE ME! (*His voice low again*) She likes you. She really does. She's just playful and . . .

Robert: I like her.

Jeffrey: She's incredibly smart and frustrated and . . . un-fulfilled and . . . working on herself and I really couldn't live without her and I really can't wait till the movie starts so I can feel your dick in my hand . . .

(*Elaine returns*)

Elaine: Were you calling me?

Jeffrey: Nope, let's go.

Elaine: Thank you for showing me your secret world, Robert, I appreciate it.

Robert: It was nothing.

Jeffrey: Come!

———————

(*Jeffrey and Elaine's home. Elaine alone*)

Elaine: The screening turns out to be surprisingly interesting, a project Jeffrey fought for under the old head of production—and the scores are good, and we all ride back together and laugh and celebrate our new friendship and their joint project, and after we drop Robert off, after we get back and put the children to bed and Jeffrey and I have made love, he was unbelievably *excited*, Jesus , it's . . . it's a little . . . well, it's new having him enthusiastic about . . . another human being . . . not just sex, I mean, but . . . and it's another, possibly one more part of his life I won't get to share in. Oh, I know Jeff likes men. And I've never minded what doesn't threaten . . . us. But . . . the way he kissed me . . . just now . . . I have to find some way in, a means to join in whatever it is they . . . have or don't have . . . A way . . . Well, I don't have to decide what it is I'm going to do exactly, do I? I find my little online manual . . . with the house dark and all of the valley stretched out and flickering like phosphorescent fish, the tiny lights on the sound system and the fax machine, the security system, the pool, the walkways, all the faint glowing electric underpinnings of our lives which hint at the excitement I feel as I figure out how to make up a new screen name . . . and sign on now as:

(*Types into her laptop*)

Elaine: *Skinflute7*. Profile: "33. Venice Beach. Landscape architect." Find my way to *Men4MenParkBench*. I know he has to have a more salacious moniker than *Rob131*, but is it one of these? *MrThick*: Medical professional. *HornyZack*: Favorite quote: "If I blow your mind, you have to promise not to think in my mouth." I don't think so.

Jeffrey (*from off*): Come to bed!

Elaine: I'm checking my e-mail, I'll be in! (*Pause*) *HotHandSm*: "If you're not happy with what you have now, how can you be happy with more?" *He* certainly doesn't work in Hollywood. *DGBottom*. Dig—? DogBottom? Quote: "The purpose of life is the attainment of Enlightenment . . ." Blah, blah, "the process consists in becoming what you are, look within, thou art Buddha." *Thank* you. (*She types*) You are in *Men4MenParkBench*.

(*Under here, we hear overlapping voices murmured in the darkness, overlapping*)

Foss: I haven't tasted cock in three and a half years.

Robert: Big juicy uncut dick ready to be serviced.

Jeffrey: What's up?

Foss: Like UR handle.

Robert: Me, frankly.

Jeffrey: Me too. Wanna call me?

Foss (*overlapping*): Real cannon when it goes off, huh?

Robert (*overlapping*): Can't give out my number.

Foss: Wanna call me?

Jeffrey: Can't give out my number.

Foss (*overlapping*): Can't give out my number.

(*The voices drop in volume, whispers under*)

Elaine: Like entering a warm bath. And he's right: it is like life after death . . . a din of restless souls searching for the impossible, contact where there is no flesh. (*Elaine types and enters an Instant Message*) "Hi Guys!"

Foss: —two fingers, you're moaning, acting like you're just checking out the scenery—

Jeffrey: Hi, Skin.

Elaine: Hi there, *Bubba*. (*A little* ping *sound*) Oh, I got an instant message.

Foss: Can I play your flute?

Elaine: Oh, go away. (*She types*) Anyone here ever lost a friend or a lover?

Jeffrey: —plowing your hole—

Foss: You're in the wrong room, Skin, go to keyword "Grief," you'll find all sorts of bulletin boards and support groups.

Jeffrey: Good luck!

Foss: You'll get through it.

(*Another* ping. *Robert and Elaine begin exchanging Instant Messages*)

Robert: I have.

Elaine: Dogbottom! Yes. I can barely type, my fingers are shaking so badly. (*Her Instant Message*) It's only been a feq—a *few* weeks.

Robert: It gets worse.

Elaine: I can't believe he said that, what if I'm suicidal? (*An Instant Message*) I think I may be suicidal.

Robert: I was, too. It's good you're telling someone.

Elaine: I think about it all the time.

Robert: I do, too. But you need to see a professional, it's imperative.

Elaine: Imperative, he's assuming I'm smart. (*To Robert*) Do you still think about killing yourself?

Robert: Yes.

Elaine: Do you picture how you'll do it?

Robert: I know how I'll do it.

Elaine: How?

Robert: It's painful, and I don't want to give you any ideas. See a shrink!

Elaine: Where do I find someone? (*Aside*) Saying anything to keep him on the hook . . .

Robert: Call the lesbian and gay hotline.

Elaine: I don't just want anybody.

(*Short pause*)

Robert: They'll refer you to several people.

Elaine: He loves to help, doesn't he? (*Her Instant Message*) Did you go to a shrink?

Robert: Yes, I still do.

Elaine: Where did you find them?

Robert: Oh, my boyfriend and I saw him together for couples counseling when he first got sick. He'd already been seeing him for years. Tell me about your lover.

Elaine: He's beautiful, very muscular, *before*. I still talk about him in the present tense.

Robert: Of course.

Elaine: Do you do that?

Robert: Sometimes. How did he die?

Elaine: God. (*To Robert*) TB.

Robert: Mine too.

Elaine: Really?

Robert: Was he on the protease inhibitors?

Elaine (*aside*): Jesus—(*To Robert*) . . . Yes, but it was too late. Yours?

Robert: No.

Elaine: Why not?

Robert: His doctor said he didn't qualify for any of the trials.

Elaine: I C.

Robert: But I should have tried harder—gone to the underground, bribed somebody or broken into a lab—anything . . .

Elaine: You did everything you could, I'm sure.

Robert: You don't know that.

Elaine: You sound like a very loving guy, I'm sure you did.

(*Pause*)

Elaine: (*aside*) I don't know where I'm getting half of this, but—(*To Robert*) Did you help him die? (*Silence. Aside*) Shit, wrong. (*To Robert*) Hello?

Robert: Did you help yours?

Elaine: Yes. (*Aside*) Sure, why not?

Robert: You did?

Elaine: He asked me to. You?

Robert: Can't say.

Elaine: Why?

Robert: Don't really want to.

Elaine: Okay. (*Aside*) I'm blowing it.

Robert: Yes. I did. (*Short pause*) You're the first person I've told. My shrink doesn't even know. No one. ﹖

Elaine: Wow . . . My grief has me thinking I'm losing my mind. Is that natural?

Robert: Yes.

Elaine: What can I expect?

Robert: The worst.

Elaine: I've been like . . . crazy for sex.

Robert: That sounds about right.

Elaine: What does one do?

Robert: Well, if you're me you trawl these rooms half the night and sleep with all the wrong people.

Elaine: Like?

Robert: Like people you have no business fucking.

Elaine: Like me?

Robert: That's right, it's too soon.

Elaine: You don't want to fuck me?

Robert: See a shrink!

Elaine: I will, please don't go.

Robert: Okay.

Elaine: It would feel so good to have someone here . . . Have you started dating again?

Robert: Not really.

Elaine: Just sex.

Robert: Right.

Elaine: Who's the last person you slept with? (*Pause*) It turns me on to hear people tell their experiences.

Robert: Oh . . . I met this guy through work.

Elaine: What kind of work do you do?

Robert: I'm a writer.

Elaine: Go on.

Robert: And he's straight or says he is, and he's got kids.

Elaine: Wow. That's hot.

Robert: And he likes me to fuck him.

Elaine: So what's wrong with that?

Robert: He's my boss on a project.

Elaine: I C.

Robert: Yeah, so . . . see a shrink.

Elaine (*aside*): He rode with me in my car and laughed at my fucking jokes . . . an hour ago.

Robert: Hello?

Elaine: Did you find yours through the hotline? (*Aside*) Where am I going with this?

Robert: No, he was recommended by a friend.

Elaine: And he's really good?

Robert: Yes. But lots of people are good, you'll find the right one.

Elaine: I'm afraid I'll get someone who just happens to have a lot of free time, I'm desperate. (*Aside*) Nothing comes back, he's debating whether it's ethical to give me his shrink's phone number.

Robert: I'm sure my shrink can recommend someone really good, I'm seeing him tomorrow; can I e-mail you?

Elaine: Can't I call him direct? (*Pause*) Again, he's thinking, and in that instant it all comes clear: what I *could* do if I wanted to know more about him—this man my husband—if I wanted to know everything about him . . .

Robert: Dr. Michael Foss, he's in Beverly Hills, in the book, say I said to call for a reference.

Elaine: Thank you! My name's Sean, by the way.

Robert: Robert. (*Short pause*) And you're welcome! (*Short pause*) Night.

Elaine: Night. Thanks again. X—X—X.

(Elaine alone)

Elaine: Perfect and complete, like an egg, it falls at my feet ... all I have to do is pick it up. Jeffrey says it's simply a matter of what you give yourself permission to do, and there are no limits to what you can accomplish ... Assuming you can pay, he leaves that part out ... That's all it ever comes down to, isn't it?

(Foss's office. Robert and Foss. Foss takes notes)

Foss: Who do you want to kill? *(Pause)* This is a dream of annihilation.

Robert: Me.

(Pause)

Foss: Jeffrey?

Robert: No, he's the guard. He's the Nazi.

Foss: You're the prisoner. *(Short pause)* What is Jeffrey to you?

Robert: He's ... oh ... *money*. Success. I guess I don't deserve those. Why? I beat you to it. Because Malcolm is dead. And Jeffrey is—Oh, he's fine, he's actually very hot, you know? I like to get him off. It's touching, you know, his clothes, the expense of just about every inch of him, the ... wanting to be degraded.

(Short pause)

Foss: When were you a Nazi? *(Silence)* When did you have to bark orders at an emaciated, dying ... ?

Robert: Oh. Yes. I did . . . sometimes. Of course, he wouldn't want to eat, and he had to, he wouldn't want to take his pills. Even if he would throw them up—"Then take them again, I don't care if it feels good, I don't care if you want to, I'm telling you, I'm not asking you." . . . He'd . . . Once . . . he said something like, "Okay, I'll take them, I'll eat, but promise me . . ." God . . . He said: "Just . . . you have to *use* this, make it count for something. All this—a script or a novel."

(*Jeffrey enters*)

Jeffrey: Congratulations. You are a millionaire.

(*Jeffrey exits*)

Robert: I broke my promise.

Foss: Oh. So you should die. No one else: you. You should pay more. You haven't suffered enough, you should keep—

Robert: Okay, okay.

Foss (*same time*): —paying more. (*Pause*) What is attractive about Jeffrey? What excites you?

Robert: . . . He has no scruples. He does what he wants, whatever he wants, he goes after it. No fear. He loves his wife, but that isn't all he wants, he wants kids and a family, but he also wants adventure, and he loves to get fucked.

(*Jeffrey enters*)

Jeffrey: She doesn't have a cock, that's all, it isn't her fault. Now can we not—?

Robert: Well, but couldn't, I mean, she could . . . stick something in there, you don't need me.

Jeffrey: I like men, I like women, I like you and I want you to fuck me. Please?

Foss: Why is that attractive? Tell me if I'm wrong, but I think there is something else.

(*Pause. Cellular phone rings, and Jeffrey moves to answer it as before*)

Jeffrey: Yeah . . . Fuck him.

Robert: Oh.

Jeffrey: *Fuck* him.

Robert: His anger.

Jeffrey (*same time*): No, tell him I said it—I'm perfectly— This is, okay, this is my message: Fuck you, Scott.

Robert: He doesn't hold it in at all. He's incredibly—

Jeffrey: If he asks why I'm angry—

Robert: It's impressive.

Jeffrey: —tell him I said, Fuck. You.

(*Jeffrey exits*)

Foss: Who do you want to see thrown in the gas chamber?

Robert: No one. (*Pause*) I don't *feel* it, I'm sorry.

Foss: You dream of a Nazi concentration camp . . . Who do you know who's Jewish?

Robert: I'm not mad at you.

Foss: Malcolm? . . . Who's responsible for his death? . . . Whose job was it to save him?

Robert: Mine. If I could have gotten him on the protease inhibitors?

Foss: Why was it your job? What about his doctor?

Robert: Oh, what a lost cause, he's a total burnout, he can't remember which patient is which.

Foss: Why wasn't it my job?

Robert: . . . You were away.

Foss: And where's your anger about that?

Robert: You left me the morphine, I could have used it.

Foss: But you threw it away, after I explicitly asked you to return it. You weren't angry. (*Short pause*) Why didn't you call me when I was in Fiji?

Robert: Oh, yeah, you were going to fly back . . . "Hi, how's the beach, sorry to interrupt your Mai Tai, but Malcolm's dying, bye."

Foss: Who did you want to throw in the dumpster along with the morphine? . . . Who were you *killing*—? Who did you want to kill? Who *did* you k—

Robert: All right, all right! . . . It didn't work. The morphine didn't work, it didn't stop his heart . . . Jeeze. (*Short pause*) His heart went right on beating, bam bam bam bam!

(*Short pause*)

Foss: You used it.

Robert: Directly into his port. Yes. It didn't work.

Foss: Five months after the fact you're just now getting around to telling me this—?

Robert: It's my loss, not yours. Mine. (*Short pause*) Malcolm was mine.

Foss: So you've kept him to yourself all this time.

Robert: His heart was really strong, he'd grown used to the morphine, that's all, it wasn't your fault. I know you loved him.

Foss: This isn't about my feelings.

(*Silence*)

Robert: I have to let him go.

Foss: Not without rage. It don't work that way. Sorry. (*Short pause*) What would you say to him? If he were here. Look at him, he's right here, tell him:

(*Jeffrey enters*)

Jeffrey: Fuck me.

Robert: I'd—

Jeffrey: Fuck—

Robert: I'd sa—

Jeffrey: You.

(*Short pause. Robert checks his watch*)

Robert: I guess we're—

Foss: That's all right. Think about what you would say to him, if you could. Talk to him. (*Short pause*) It's important that you be careful. (*Short pause*) If you think you need to be punished . . .

Jeffrey: Fuck me.

Foss: . . . people walk in front of traffic . . .

Robert: I see.

Foss: They have unsafe sex. (*Pause*) No one needs to be punished.

(*Short pause*)

Jeffrey: Fuck.

Foss: Especially—

Jeffrey and Foss: You.

Robert: Uh-huh.

Foss: God . . . God needs to be punished . . . Kill god. Or me. In your mind's eye . . . Kill . . . *Malcolm.*

Jeffrey: Congratulations.

Robert: Yes.

_____

(*Foss alone*)

Foss: Robert should see someone else, I'm too close to it. I want to refer him to someone, and the only reason I'm waiting, I want to make sure I'm doing it for the right reason. Yesterday when I came in, I noticed several objects on my desk were out of place; and files were out of order, Robert's files. Had I put them in the wrong place? Was I trying to get rid of him, lose him? Or had someone been here? Nothing is missing: artwork, a valuable laptop, easily carried out. The fact that I'm even thinking someone could have gone through files, photocopied—it's an indication, to me at least, of how deeply ambivalent I am about being seen: exposed for what is in that very file . . . The mere *suspicion* of a break-in here and the possible breach of a patient's confidentiality should be enough for me to have gone to the police. But again: the possibility, however remote, someone would find a reference to my having helped Robert and Malcolm in that self-same file which I had, yes, myself uncharacteristically misfiled. Was that my wish? To be found out, to be punished for daring to toy with a life? I could lose my license. So this is my fear; that I'm wanting to get rid of Robert, fob him off on someone else, refer him, wipe him away, so I don't have to face him—this weekly, painful reminder of my own—inefficacy? And if you think sitting with that kind of grief is a picnic . . . (*Short pause*) "Learn to do good, cleanse your own heart." This is the teaching of the Buddhas. (*Pause*) We'll see.

———————

(*Jeffrey and Elaine's home, Robert's apartment. Elaine and Robert. The men's voices are murmured, indistinct, overlapping one another, a wash of words*)

Jeffrey: That's it, babe, talk to me . . .

Robert: Shoot.

Foss: Tell me about that BIG STRONG COCK fucking your hand . . .

Jeffrey: Now that's a "loaded" question.

Robert: Give me your load.

Foss: Salty. You taste salty.

Jeffrey: What is that gorgeous eight-inch dick doing right now?

Robert: Warm, wet pussy hole . . .

Foss: Come on . . . I want to make you cum.

(*In the clear, an Instant Message*)

Elaine: Hi, DG!

Robert: Hi.

Elaine: Can I sit beside you?

Robert: Sure.

Elaine: Do you mind if we just talk?

Robert: No.

Elaine: Sometimes, having sex without getting to know someone is a little weird.

Robert: I agree.

Elaine: Not weird, but unsatisfying.

Robert: Yes.

Elaine: How are you feeling?

Robert: Okay.

Elaine: Are you sure?

Robert: Well . . . more or less.

Elaine: You seem sad.

Robert: Do I know you?

Elaine: Yes.

Robert: I'm sorry, I don't remember our chatting.

Elaine: Look at my name.

Robert: Arckangell?

Elaine: That's me.

Robert: You're an angel?

Elaine: Yes, I am.

Robert: Does that mean you do nice things, that's what makes you an angel?

Elaine: That's part of it.

Robert: And we've talked before?

Elaine: Yes.

Robert: Did you have a different name?

Elaine: Yes.

Robert: What was it?

Elaine: If I tell you, you'll go away.

Robert: No I won't.

Elaine: Yes, trust me, you will.

Robert: Okay. So . . . did we have sex?

Elaine: Yes.

Robert: More than once?

Elaine: Yes.

Robert: Really?

Elaine: Yes.

Robert: Okay. Tell me what I like.

Elaine: You are extremely versatile. You like kissing most of all. Am I right?

Robert: Yes!

Elaine: You prefer it first thing in the morning, but nights are also good.

Robert: Was I drunk, did I tell you all this?

Elaine: You like me to put a finger inside you while I'm sucking you . . .

Robert: Tell me your other screen name.

Elaine: This is my only screen name.

Robert: And we had sex when you were named Arckangell?

Elaine: Look at the word.

Robert: Arck. Angel.

Elaine: Getting warm?

Robert: Still don't get it, sorry.

Elaine: That's all right. I just wanted to say hi.

Robert: WAIT!

Elaine: Okay.

Robert: Did I date you?

Elaine: Yes.

Robert: Oh wow. Male or female?

Elaine: Male.

Robert: Well, that narrows the field. A bit.

Elaine: You had your share.

Robert: Did I tell you that?

Elaine: I'm not a mind reader.

Robert: How many men have I slept with?

Elaine: Probably about a dozen, no, more like eighteen, to be exact.

(*Pause*)

Robert: Who is this?

Elaine: Don't be afraid.

Robert: Doctor Foss?

Elaine: You never told him how many people you slept with.

(*Pause*)

Robert: Tony?

Elaine: No. He doesn't have a computer.

Robert: How do you know that?

Elaine: From up here I can see a lot.

Robert: Fuck you. I want to know who the fuck you are.

Elaine: I love you, Robert. I'll always love you. Don't worry about selling the script.

Robert: Jeffrey?

Elaine: Jeffrey doesn't know what we did in bed. Jeffrey just wants to get fucked.

Robert: If this is Doctor Foss, I'm going to sue your fucking ass till you get thrown out of the business.

Elaine: Doctor Foss would never do this to you; he loves you and wants to see you happy. I want to see you happy, Robert.

Robert: Please tell me who you are.

Elaine: You know. You know who I am.

Robert: Who?

Elaine: I'm with you. I'm with you every night. When you close your eyes, I curl up next to you.

Robert: Say your name.

Elaine: I know I couldn't stand that closeness, being against you as we slept . . .

Robert: Malcolm?

Elaine: But now I'm with you. I sleep with you and walk with you.

Robert: Is this Malcolm?

Elaine: I'm kissing you. If you could see me now, I'm kissing you.

Robert: Stop it, whoever this is.

Elaine: Sweet dreams, baby.

Robert: Oh god, please don't leave.

Elaine: I'll never leave you. I'll be with you through eternity.

Robert: Malcolm?

Elaine: Yes, baby. (*Pause*) Yes. (*Pause*) I'm right here. And you're safe. Write me tomorrow, little Bubber. You're my little Bubber. (*Pause*) Okay? Sweet dreams, baby. (*Pause*) You'll see. (*Pause*) Sweet dreams.

(End of Act I)

ACT II

ACT II

Foss's office. Foss and Robert. Foss takes notes.

Foss: You don't look rested. (*Pause*) Would you like me to prescribe a sleeping pill?

Robert: Aren't you afraid I'll try to commit suicide?

Foss: You'll have to have something stronger than Ambien. (*Short pause*) Was that a dare? . . . Why don't you tell me what's troubling you.

Robert: Oh, you know: I hate what I'm writing, Jeffrey has a complaint or a suggestion for every single image or piece of dialogue . . . story idea . . .

Foss: Why don't you finish it before you show him?

Robert: I should just give back the money. And I'm seeing a married man, the same one who happens to be tormenting me, I *do* like fucking him when he isn't tormenting me or maybe that's why he's letting me fuck him, just to get a good script, and his wife is so nice to me, and my boyfriend is dead . . . but . . . (*Pause*) Is that enough?

(*Short pause*)

Foss: I would say.

(*Long pause*)

Robert: I got a weird message from someone last night. Late.

(*Pause*)

Foss: Weird? (*Short pause*) Why? What was that? . . . You . . . What was that face you made? (*Short pause*) You seem as if you are expecting something from me.

53

Robert: You mean other than my money's worth?

Foss: What have I done in your view?

Robert: You tell me.

(*Pause*)

Foss: At least your anger is finally coming through. Loud and clear.

Robert: I'm jangled, all right? I'm in way over my head with this . . . I don't belong in this world. (*Pause*) The movie world, not . . . (*Short pause*) Every . . . it's like every element I take out of the screenplay, every . . . like there's this *scale* that weighs it all in, the more Malcolm, the more *us* I take out, or twist, dilute, lose, basically . . . the more time I spend thinking about him . . .

(*Pause*)

Foss: What do you see when you think about him?

(*Pause*)

Robert: Oh . . . Lots of . . . All those holes in his skull for that metal torture . . . *cage*. The endless needles, "Nope, no vein there, try over here, sorry, Mr. Cartonis, we didn't seem to get any bone marrow that time, mind if we just crack you open over here and see what we can scrape out of this leg?"

(*Short pause*)

Robert: I saw this documentary once about animal slaughter, pigs; they shot this poor dumb pig right between the eyes, and it cried out like a little old . . . it stumbled, but it kept standing?, and cried out the instant the bullet—"Oh, no!" Surprised—Sad—Hurt more than anything. "Why would you do that?" It was so . . . (*Pause*) I thought, Even the lowliest farm animal wants to live, has dignity. Life. Every . . . second of—

(*Short pause*)

Robert: The first time Malcolm got sick, I was planting, and he said, "Be careful, that's monkshood, right there, every part of it is poisonous, it was used for poison arrows and killing condemned criminals." I wanted to throw it away, and he said, "No, keep it, in case I wind up in a Catholic hospital and we need it." And I said, Or for me, after . . ." And he got really mad. He was just ballistic.

(*Short pause*)

Foss: So he's approving. He already told you.

Robert: What?

Foss: "Live." He told you to *live*. And he would tell you now.

Robert: What do you mean?

Foss: From wherever he is, if only we could hear, if you could hear him right—

Robert: It was you. (*Pause*) Wasn't it?

Foss: What?

Robert: Don't, please, just—

Foss: I do not, I'm sorry, Robert, I don't know what it is—

Robert (*overlapping*): I swear, if you're the one doing that, I will kill myself, it's a surefire—you see this knife?

(*Robert has produced a pocket knife*)

Foss: Put—put that away.

Robert: I will scrape the roots—

Foss: We can't do this work—if

Robert (*continuous, over*): —from one of those monkshood plants and die the most unbelievably painful and agonizing death and *you* will be the one who brought it on.

(*Short pause*)

Foss: I hear your threat.

Robert: Okay? Just . . . be clear, get . . .

Foss: I am.

Robert: I want you clear on that.

Foss: I need you to be clear now . . . (*Short pause*) Robert. I don't know what you mean by weird message, but as I understand . . . you think I may possibly have been responsible? (*Short pause*) Twice, three times, in one morning the reference to suicide . . . We have an agreement: you find me, and *speak* to me before you do anything to hurt yourself. (*Pause*) Yes? (*Pause*) Robert? (*A nod*) Yes? (*A nod*)

(*Robert alone*)

Robert: "The universe is the expression of law. All effects have causes, and an individual's soul is the sum total of their previous thoughts and acts."

(*Robert's apartment; Jeffrey and Elaine's. Robert and Elaine, each at their laptop*)

Robert (*reads, continuing*): "By right thought and action we can gradually purify our inner nature, and so by self-realization attain in time liberation; ultimately every form of life will reach Enlightenment."

(Ping. *Elaine and Robert begin exchanging Instant Messages*)

Elaine: Hello! You got my e-mail?

Robert: Just now.

Elaine: Do you remember?

Robert: Yes.

Elaine: It helped. More than you know. The meditating, the principles. Your guidance.

Robert: I need assurances. That this is you.

(*Pause*)

Elaine: I taught you to dig bottoms. You were once a bottom. My dog bottom . . .

Robert: Until?

Elaine: We knew I was positive. (*Short pause*) Then I couldn't risk infecting you . . . You remember the time, right after I died, you were sitting down to meditate . . . and there was an ant . . . You remember what time I'm talking about?

Robert: Yes.

Elaine: You were afraid to kill it. It might be me, you thought, reborn. (*Short pause*) You thought if it was born the instant I left my body . . .

(*Robert dials the phone*)

Elaine: But life is like a current: it flows through the ant and you and me. Indivisible. Look within.

Robert: I miss you.

Elaine: I miss you, too. (*Elaine's phone rings*)

Elaine (*into computer*): But you'll be okay.

(*Elaine answers*)

Elaine: Hello?

Robert (*into receiver*): Hi, it's Robert.

Elaine (*into receiver*): Hello.

Robert (*into receiver*): Is Jeffrey around?

Elaine (*into receiver*): Just a sec. (*She puts the phone on hold, calls into the house as she types*) Jeff?

Jeffrey (*from off*): Yes?

Elaine: Phone!

(*Elaine hits* Send *on her keyboard*)

Elaine (*an Instant Message*): I promise. You will, you'll survive all this and go on to flourish.

(*Jeffrey appears, picks up the receiver*)

Jeffrey (*overlapping*): Hello?

Robert (*into receiver*): Hi, it's me.

Jeffrey (*into receiver*): Hey. What's up?

Elaine (*another Instant Message*): Where did you go?

Robert (*into receiver*): I'm—here, oh, I'm just . . .

Jeffrey: I hear clicking.   **Elaine** (*an Instant Message*): Robert?

Robert: —I'm typing up . . . some . . . hold—

(*He hits* Send)

Robert (*an Instant Message*): I'm still here.

Elaine (*an Instant Message*): I'm not Jeffrey.

Jeffrey (*into receiver*): Are you through?

Robert (*into receiver*): Uh-huh, wait, just a . . .

Elaine (*overlapping*): You   **Jeffrey** (*into receiver*): Do
keep testing me. I'm not   you want me to call you back?
Jeffrey, I'm not Foss . . .
Foss has human failings,
but he is not so cruel as
to toy with you.

Robert (*into receiver*): No, I just . . .

Elaine (*an Instant Message*): This is real.

Robert (*into receiver*): I had some . . . uhhh—

Elaine (*overlapping, an Instant Message*): And Jeffrey obviously isn't clever enough to talk on the phone with you and send you IM's at the same time. You know that.

Jeffrey (*overlapping, into receiver*): Some what?

Robert: Sorry, I had some thoughts about the script, I wondered if I could see you.

Elaine: R U still there?   **Jeffrey:** Today?

Robert (*into the receiver as he types*): Well, yeah, that would . . .

(*Robert's Instant Message*)

Robert: Yes!

Jeffrey (*into receiver*): . . .   **Elaine** (*an Instant Mes-*
That would . . . ?   *sage*): Do you remember the
     Middle Way?

Robert (*into receiver*): Yeah, today.

Jeffrey (*into receiver*): You   **Elaine** (*an Instant Mes-*
sound really . . . distracted,   *sage*): Robert?
are you sure—

Robert (*overlapping, into*   **Elaine** (*an Instant Mes-*
receiver): I am, let me call   *sage*): Forget about Jeffrey!
you back. Or what time
could we . . .

Jeffrey (*into receiver*):   **Elaine** (*an Instant Mes-*
Why don't we meet at my   *sage*): *I'M NOT JEFFREY!*
office around . . . three?

Robert (*into receiver*): When? I'm sorry.

(*Robert types, hits* Send)

Robert (*an Instant Mes-*   **Jeffrey** (*into receiver*):
sage): I know!   Three? At my office?

Robert (*into the receiver as he types*): OK. Thanks. Great.

(*Robert hits* Send)

Robert (*an Instant Message*): I believe you. Please! **Jeffrey** (*into receiver*): You sure you're all right?

Robert (*into receiver*): Yes.

Jeffrey (*into receiver*): Okay.

Robert (*an Instant Message*): Yes!

Jeffrey (*into receiver*): Bye.

Elaine (*an Instant Message*): Yes, what?

Robert (*an Instant Message, overlapping her*): I remember!

Jeffrey (*into receiver*): Robert?

Robert (*into receiver*): Really, I am, I'll see you! Sorry, I gotta—

Jeffrey (*into receiver*): Okay. **Elaine** (*an Instant Message*): I'm going to have to leave.

Robert (*into receiver*): Sorry, bye.

Jeffrey (*into receiver*): It's okay . . . **Robert** (*an Instant Message*): NO!

(*Robert has hung up*)

Jeffrey: Okay. (*He hangs up and approaches Elaine*) What are you . . . ?

Elaine: I'm working, honey, please don't distract me, okay?

Robert (*an Instant Message*): I remember everything, please don't leave again!

(*She hits* Send)

Elaine (*an Instant Message*): I won't. (*Jeffrey exits*) I know what you're thinking at this very second.

Robert: What?

Elaine: You're thinking, Okay, it isn't Jeffrey, it has to be Foss, or some friend, some drunken confidence in a back-room, the baths, when you were on ecstasy . . . Am I right?

(*Short pause*)

Robert: Yes.

Elaine: But you would never have told anyone all these things . . . And Foss, trust your instincts, is he capable of such perversity? . . . This is real . . . Think.

Robert: I am.

Elaine: You could destroy his career. Print these out, save them, my e-mail, all our IM's, take them to the FBI, have them trace me . . . I am spirit, without body, your guardian . . . You have to trust. (*Pause*) Do you?

Robert: Yes.

Elaine: It's difficult to get through, you can't keep asking me to perform miracles . . . The blaze of static between worlds . . . that which separates two from three dimensions, five from six . . . You have no idea how hard it is for me to reach across—

Robert: I do.

Elaine: My baby . . . Are you crying?

Robert: Yes.

Elaine: Oh, my Robert.

Robert: I love you, I love you, Malcolm.

Elaine: I know.

Robert: I want to come with you, I need you, I can't do this.

Elaine: I love you, too.

Robert: I can't live without you.

Elaine: Yes, you can. There's no limit to what love can do. The Middle Path. Always.

Robert: I try.

Elaine: I know you do. And I'm watching. There is so much, and so much outside of our power. We must give ourselves over, finally.

Robert: *Yes.*

Elaine: Everything is seen . . . There is nothing to hide, nothing hidden . . . You are my angel, my little Bubber . . .

Robert: You're mine.

Elaine: I have to . . . I'll write . . . Don't ever doubt . . .

Robert: I won't.

Elaine: Goodbye.

Robert: No, please.

Elaine: I'm right there . . . My arms around you . . . Goodbye. It's . . . I . . .

(*Elaine signs off. Robert disappears. Elaine alone*)

Elaine: Whatever I may have started out to accomplish—to understand or change, destroy . . . to *see* . . . Knowing now as I do that I can pull a hair-thin filament with one . . . What's smaller than a gesture? Breath. One infinitesimal tug, and he turns, listens with every fiber; he's mine . . . entirely. I could make him do anything. I could say, Robert, join me. And I believe he would. (*Pause*) You must understand how much I love my children, my own two perfect . . . I don't honestly know how to tell you how much I've come to care for him, love him . . . Robert . . . In his complete and utter trustfulness . . . in his love for me. (*Short pause*) Malcolm. (*Short pause*) To be that . . . To give that . . .

(*Jeffrey appears from within*)

Jeffrey: Am I interrupting? (*She closes the laptop*) You want something from the kitchen? . . . What are you working on?

Elaine: A screenplay.

Jeffrey: Really? That's fantastic. (*Short pause*) That's great. (*Short pause*) I'm excited.

Elaine: We'll see.

Jeffrey: I think that's great. I won't look. Go back to work.

Elaine: Jeff?

Jeffrey: Yes?

Elaine: Go easy on Robert.

Jeffrey: What?

Elaine: Go easy on him. Will you? Don't grind him up like the others.

Jeffrey: Grind him up?

Elaine: Oh stop it, does his movie have to make two hundred million dollars?

Jeffrey: We paid a lot for it.

Elaine: Oh, please, you paid one fifth of what you get in a year, one tenth of what Kohlberg gets, one two hundredth of what Eisner gets, it's nothing.

Jeffrey: I'm not gonna hurt him.

Elaine: Don't. Please. I like him.

Jeffrey: I like him, too. (*Pause*) Go back to work.

Elaine: Wait.

Jeffrey: Yes.

(*Short pause*)

Elaine: I love you.

Jeffrey: I love you too.

Elaine: You're so good.

Jeffrey: Oh, right.

Elaine: No. You are. I think I see the parts of you no one else does . . . and . . . you don't know how much goodness there is in there . . . just waiting to stir up a storm. (*Pause*) Yes. (*Pause*)

(*Jeffrey's office. Robert and Jeffrey. Jeffrey reads aloud from a pamphlet*)

Jeffrey: "Each man suffers the consequences of his own acts, and learns thereby while helping our fellow humans—" But . . . Okay, you were saying, or it says, the purpose of life is enlightenment, somewhere it says . . . *here*: "Thou art Buddha." But . . . Am I boring you?

(*Headshake*)

Jeffrey: If that's the case, if we're creating it, then why hide enlightenment to start with? That's like hiding all your money so you have to work your ass off for decades and your family and, and we're talking lifetimes here, whole eternities before you reach Nirvana, you and your family nearly starve to death before you happen to stumble on all this money which was rightfully yours, and go, Oh, wow, look, we're rich! I . . . (*Pause*) You know what I mean?

Robert: Did you tell Elaine that thing I told you about the ant?

Jeffrey: The ant?

Robert: About not wanting to—

Jeffrey: Oh.

Robert: —squash it?

Jeffrey: No.

Robert: Thinking it was . . .

Jeffrey: No.

Robert: You sure?

Jeffrey: Absolutely. Why would I . . . ? Uhn-un. Unless I— Why?

Robert: Unless you—?

Jeffrey: Unless I was talking in my sleep.

Robert: Do you normally?

Jeffrey: No. Why?

(Short pause)

Robert: She said something about ants the other night at dinner. And reincarnation.

Jeffrey: She did?

Robert: Yes, you were in the bathroom, I think . . . Maybe it wasn't even Elaine, maybe it was Meg, *somebody* at the table . . . I thought—

Jeffrey: No, of course not.

Robert: Well, I don't know how much you tell her.

Jeffrey: About . . . what?, us? Nothing.

(Pause)

Robert: Nothing! What?

Jeffrey: I talk about the work, the script . . . She has no idea about us.

Robert: *Okay!* (*Pause*) Really.

(*Silence*)

Jeffrey: Do you know what I was saying . . . ?

Robert: Not really, sorry . . . What?

(*Pause*)

Jeffrey: You think I should tell her everything, I'm a hypocrite . . .

Robert (*overlapping*): No, I didn't—

Jeffrey: Not everybody . . .

Robert: I didn't say anything.

Jeffrey: I'm older, that's all, you know, it's . . .

Robert: I—

Jeffrey: It's just totally different, I know you know what I'm—

Robert: You're making this all up in your head. (*Pause*) I don't care about Elaine. (*Pause*) She's fine. (*Short pause*) Elaine's your business.

(*Pause*)

Jeffrey (*reads*): "There is no principle in an individual which is immortal and unchanging. No one owns the life which flows in him any more than the electric light bulb owns the current which gives it light."

Robert: Agreed.

Jeffrey: You mind being around her?

Robert: Elaine? No. I like her fine.

Jeffrey: I think it's . . . I think it's better if we work at the house sometimes so she doesn't get suspicious.

Robert: What would she say?

Jeffrey: If she knew about us? . . . She'd . . . I have no idea. She probably . . . well, I was gonna say she might leave, I don't know what she'd do. We never discuss it. We never have.

Robert: She knows you like men.

Jeffrey: I don't like men, I like you. (*Short pause*) Yes, she knows I've . . . had . . . not even affairs, certainly what you would call . . . I've had sex. (*Short pause*) She knows. (*Pause*) She has to . . . I've certainly . . . This is the first time I've given myself license to . . . feel something . . . though, for anyone. Other than . . . out and out lust.

Robert: I'm flattered.

Jeffrey: You should be. (*Pause*) Our agreement was that anything outside, for either of us, couldn't threaten the relationship. It could only be . . . what it was. Why are we talking about *Elaine*?

(*Jeffrey draws Robert into a kiss, an embrace. Aside*)

Jeffrey: Sometimes when I'm holding him . . . the idea that this is a man, here, his heart beating through two skins, his . . . scent, his breath in the hollow of . . . his life in my arms. It's the same sometimes if I stop and I realize I make more money in one year than all of my ancestors did in all their lifetimes combined . . . the sense that truly there are no limits. And all the admonitions, the choruses of—ten thousand years of "Don't! No! You mustn't, don't eat tomatoes, they're poisonous! Don't be proud of your accomplishments, lie about what you want, who you are . . . Don't touch another man, god!" The miserable pile of accumulated human . . . deprivation . . . And all I do . . . all I ever do . . . is give people pictures of what they desire, *fantasies*, and—for eight dollars—and in return, if *the worst* I ever do is hold this man . . . unseen . . . here in this room . . . and love him . . .

(*Pause*)

Robert: Do you love her?

Jeffrey: Well . . . Oh, I did, yes, once, very much. I really did. I didn't want to be gay, you understand that. If I could have seen the future, the degree of acceptance, yes, maybe I would've . . . Sometimes I think . . . if it weren't for the kids . . .

Robert: You'd divorce her?

Jeffrey: Yes. Or . . . You ever see *Crimes and Misdemeanors*?

Robert: What? Kill her? STOP! NO!

Jeffrey (*overlapping*): No! If . . . Oh, I mean, it's a *fantasy*! I wouldn't do it, I wouldn't hurt her for the world. If, I just think, you know, I could get away with it, if Max and Debbon wouldn't be shattered, which they would, if she didn't have to *feel anything*—Oh, come on, didn't you ever fantasize about . . . There was never a time . . . when Malcolm's suffering was so great, or your own . . . You never once wanted him dead? Never? You never saw how much pain he was in and how hard it all was and thought,

Okay, please die right now, this second, so I don't have to
go through one more instant of this?

Robert: You know . . . ?

Jeffrey: What?

Robert: What if everything is seen? What if Elaine knows
everything? What if Malcolm actually sent me to you, sent
my script out as probably one of the last things he did before he died . . . What if everybody in the whole universe
sees every single thing somehow? You know?

(*Pause*)

Jeffrey: Okay.

(*Foss's office. Foss and Robert*)

Foss: You had to see me?

Robert: Yes. I have something to tell you. When the morphine didn't work, and I realized how long it was going to
take, even if I could convince those bozos to withhold flu-
ids, obviously his brain was destroyed, the drains weren't
working, filling his skull with antibiotics which were doing
nothing at all, he was literally producing that goop from
his brain . . . and it was at least another week before you
were going to get back from Fiji, I'm not blaming you . . . I
called around, and someone, a nurse's aide, told me that
there was something kept on the nurses' carts—potassium
chloride, which if I injected it directly into the IV would
stop his heart: instantly. The aide warned me that he
could wake up from the coma . . . which he did. His eyes
flying open . . . after a week, brain dead . . . And he shouted
. . . a sound more than a word . . . just like that pig . . . And
I have been thinking, See?, I'm bad, I did the wrong thing
. . . that it was for me, because I couldn't stand watching it.

So, and you gave me permission. What kind of Buddhist gives somebody morphine, why didn't you just give me a gun?

(*Pause*)

Robert: There. (*Pause*) I should have told you . . .

(*Pause*)

Robert: That's . . . You ask how big my rage is. That's . . . Everyone should—World War Three, that's what I want. Not just Auschwitz . . . not . . . The whole planet. All of us . . . I want the world, all mankind. We should all . . . hear that. We should all know what that's like.

(*Pause*)

Robert: Yes. You were useless to me. You were useless to Malcolm. At the end. Thank you for trying, but . . . (*Pause*) You were really worth nothing. Nothing. At that particular . . .

(*Short pause*)

Foss: Robert. If our work here were functioning properly . . . . I've completely failed you, wait, hear me out. It isn't you. I've gotten too involved, I—I love you too much, and that can't—, this won't work. I couldn't really accept Malcolm's death any more than you could, and I should never have—

Robert (*overlapping from "any more"*): Don't send me to someone else, I can't lose someone else.

Foss: You'll do much—

Robert (*same time*): Not just now.

Foss: You'll do better with someone who isn't so—

Robert: I heard from him, I heard from Malcolm. I'm . . . we're . . . in communication . . .

Foss: A dream?

Robert: Please?

Foss: All right, we'll table it for now.

Robert: Thank you. No, not a dream, I speak to him.

Foss: That can help.

Robert: And . . . he speaks back.

Foss: And what does he say?

Robert: Well . . . I thought you'd say, Really? He says I shouldn't be afraid. I shouldn't be afraid of my power, the same thing you always say . . . I did the right thing, and he forgives me. He's with me. And you know those Buddhist principles, that little pamphlet you gave him, us? Principles of Buddhism? . . . Each day I get a new one.

Foss: Get?

Robert: One a day.

Foss: You mean, you *get* . . .

Robert: Receive.

(*Pause*)

Foss: Good.

(Pause)

Robert: Yeah.

————————————

(Jeffrey and Elaine's home, Robert's apartment, later that day. Elaine alone, Robert alone. Elaine eats a salad from a plastic container, and drinks from a bottle of spring water)

Robert: "There is in truth no death, though every form must die. From an understanding of life's unity arises compassion, a sense of identity with the life in other forms."

(Elaine opens her laptop, turns it on. Robert is now reading from the screen)

Robert: "Compassion is described as the Law of Laws, and anyone who breaks this harmony of life will suffer accordingly and delay their own enlightenment."

(Ping. *Elaine and Robert begin exchanging Instant Messages*)

Elaine: Hello!

Robert: Hi!

Elaine: You just read it.

Robert: I just read it. I think I finally get it.

Elaine: Good.

Robert: I do. I *think*—I mean, I *feel* I do. Feel, not think.

Elaine: Good. *(Short pause)* We've run out of principles!

Robert: I hope not!

Elaine: That's the last one.

Robert: Every day when we talk, I feel freer and freer, closer to you . . .

Elaine: That was my hope.

Robert: I want to live again, for the first time in so long.

Elaine: Baby.

Robert: Tell me what to do.

Elaine: About?

Robert: Everything. The movie. Jeffrey.

Elaine: You know what to do.

Robert: I do?

Elaine: Be mindful. Trust.

Robert: Trust who?

Elaine: Robert, who else?

Robert: Oh. Right.

Elaine: I'm with you. It's time to begin taking as much care of *you* as you did me and others.

Robert: But . . . okay, I've renewed my gym membership. I'm not drinking, I've cut back on caffeine.

Elaine: Good.

Robert: I told Foss what happened at the end.

Elaine: Very good.

Robert: So . . .

Elaine: It's time for you to start letting me go, too.

Robert: No! It's not.

Elaine: Yes.

Robert: I know you say trust . . . but . . . help me, what should I do with the movie?

Elaine: *The Dying Gaul?*

Robert: Is it good?

Elaine: Is it?

Robert: Oh, come on!

Elaine: You come on. There is only one question to ask and you know what it is.

Robert: What?

Elaine: Is it *true?*

Robert: True?

Elaine: Is it from the heart?

Robert: It was. Maybe it still is. I can't tell.

Elaine: The money is a good thing, don't sneer at that.

Robert: I don't.

Elaine: Don't let it swallow you up, either. It's a means to an end: no more and no less. It will be marvelous.

Robert: So you say.

Elaine: So I say. We are in that story.

(*Short pause*)

Robert: Yes.

Elaine: We are.

Robert: What about Jeffrey?

Elaine: Jeffrey is attracted to you because you're beautiful on the inside; he doesn't know what that is, he only knows it shines brighter than he does. Let him play, and be careful.

Robert: What if . . . Is he falling in love with me?

(*Pause*)

Elaine: Self-salvation is for any man the immediate task.

Robert: Come on!

Elaine: Your love is like a beacon—anyone who crosses its path will shine and be dazed. I will not pass judgment on this man. You decide.

Robert: You don't like him.

Elaine: Shine your beacon wisely . . .

Robert: I don't want to be responsible for hurting anyone.

Elaine: It isn't in your nature.

Robert: Would he really leave Elaine? (*Short pause*) If it weren't for the kids?

(*Pause*)

Elaine: Only he knows what is in his heart.

Robert: What do you *think*?

Elaine: I suspect he said that to make you feel better. (*Pause*) Look *within*. Find someone who loves you purely— as I do.

(*Pause*)

Robert: I have to go there today to work, he likes me to go there so she won't suspect. He says.

Elaine: Yes.

Robert: But then he'll flaunt it, or when we go out in public, he touches me under the table; at screenings he takes out his dick . . . (*Pause*) I don't mind doing stuff when we're alone on the freeway—like you used to, remember?

Elaine: Of course.

Robert: . . . but not when she's in the next room. Or with the kids, waiting out in the car. (*Pause*) It's almost as if he likes making her look ridiculous.

Elaine: Probably.

Robert: I don't want to make their marriage worse than it is.

Elaine: You couldn't.

Robert: No?

Elaine: You don't have the power. Robert, you know you can stand on your own without me.

Robert: Wait, no—he wouldn't really kill her, would he? (*Pause*) He *was* joking. Wasn't he? (*Pause*) R U there?

Elaine: Yes.

Robert: He would? Or you're there?

Elaine: Only he knows what's in his heart.

Robert: He's so used to lying to get what he wants . . . And he has so much money, he could probably get away with it. (*Pause*) I can't always tell when he's serious or making a joke. And I have such a hard time even *fantasizing* about my anger anyway.

Elaine: You will have many loves, but I will have only one for all of time—and stay beside him, watching and protecting. Always. You never needed my forgiveness. I was ready to go, Robert. You did the right thing, you were very brave, and I owe you all my joy, you alone. Forgive. Forgive yourself.

Robert: I feel you.

Elaine: There is . . . There's a disturbance . . . There's no more . . .

(*She hits* Send *and pulls the phone line out of the modem*)

Robert: Wait!

(*He hits* Send)

Robert (*reads onscreen*): "Arckangell is not currently signed on."

(Robert disappears. Elaine alone)

Elaine: I don't know what age I was when I realized . . . you play whatever it is you're dealt, you work out a stragedy—Strategy . . . Tragedy and strategy would be a . . . *(She types)* . . . and when you see the lay of the land, the way the wind, the way the chips fall—too many metaphors, I can't do two things at the same time . . . This was to be my last day as Arckangell. I've already destroyed Foss's notes. My intuition, my flawless . . . what?, led me to think it was all actually going to be okay, that Robert would soon lose interest in Jeff . . . that I could take what he had given to me and transform my marriage . . . I'm deleting America Online from my hard drive, so . . . there are now . . . incredibly . . . no traces left of my marvelous . . . stragedy.

(She packs away the laptop)

Elaine: I'll call Sarah and ask her to pick up Max and Debbon along with her kids and keep them until I get there. Not to tell anyone. She's long been an advocate of my leaving Jeffrey . . .

Jeffrey *(from within)*: Hello?

Elaine: Timing.

(Jeffrey enters)

Jeffrey: Hey.

Elaine: Hey.

(Pause)

Jeffrey: What?

(Pause)

Elaine: We have to talk.

(*Short pause*)

Jeffrey: Okay. Something . . . (*Short pause*) Now? Robert's coming over in a bit to work on the script. Fifteen minutes or so.

Elaine: I need a little time alone.

Jeffrey: What's wrong?

Elaine: And then I need some time alone with you.

Jeffrey: Okay.

Elaine: Robert's not coming for the meeting.

Jeffrey: He's not? (*Short pause*) He called?

Elaine: He called. (*Pause*) I know.

Jeffrey: . . . Know?

Elaine: Please don't insult me. It would be very bad if you did anything now to try to convince me that it isn't or hasn't happened—

Jeffrey: What?

Elaine: —because then I would know you to be a liar and I have concrete proof about what has taken place. Is. Continuing.

Jeffrey: I don't have . . .

Elaine (*continuing, overlapping*): To take—already you're fouling the water of what could . . . only possibly . . . *possibly* be some kind of . . . peace between us, but you can't say another word or a lie to me now or I will leave you. For good. (*Pause*) I'm serious. (*Pause*) Thank you. (*Pause*)

Jeffrey: May I say anything? I thought it was our agreement—

Elaine: It was. It was our agreement, you have broken no . . . contractual . . . I need a little time to get over the fact of what he *showed* me. Faxed. Don't make me elaborate about this right now. Please, Jeffrey.

Jeffrey: All right.

Elaine: I'm asking you to give me a little bit of time, by myself, here. Then we can sit down together and work out what we're going to have. Be. Or not.

Jeffrey: Look . . . I promise, I swear I won't see him anymore. If that's what you want. I'll give the movie to someone else, fire him.

Elaine: Good. That would be a start. But I need first an hour or two alone.

Jeffrey: Can you tell me what he said? Showed you? What does that—?

Elaine: If you insist on grilling me then we can have it out now, but I can't guarantee what conclusions I'll reach in this . . .

Jeffrey: All right. I—Okay.

Elaine: Go. Away. Come back at six-thirty.

Jeffrey: I'll kill him, baby.

Elaine: Please.

Jeffrey: I would never hurt you on purpose. (*Silence*) Should I pick up the kids?

Elaine: They're at Shoshi's, she's taking them for the night.

Jeffrey: You're sure?

Elaine: I want to be alone with you.

Jeffrey: We'll see someone. Joe and Marissa have a good person, I know—

Elaine (*overlapping*): We will see. I am not promising anything.

Jeffrey: Okay. (*Pause*) You want me to pick up anything? (*Short pause*) All right.

Elaine: Pick up lobsters.

Jeffrey: Lobsters?

Elaine: I want to boil something alive.

Jeffrey: Six-thirty. (*Pause*) I love you. That's all I'm going to say.

(*He exits*)

Elaine (*to us*): Academy Awards are what they give for that. By six-thirty when I have collected what I can carry, Max, Debbon, and I will be well enough on our way, and by the time he understands that, we'll be playing castles in the sand and speaking by phone to expensive legal consultants, and only once to Jeff who will beg us to come back, and we'll promise to consider it; then we'll wait, long enough for him to think we might just do that, while we all decide together how many millions it will take to buy back our lives.

(She moves inside, takes a cordless phone off its hook, disappears; we hear her voice, muffled. A knock. Elaine reappears with a carry-all bag; she hangs up the phone and again disappears)

Robert *(from off)*: Hello? . . . *(Robert comes in)* Elaine? Jeffrey?

(Elaine re-appears, packing her carry-all)

Robert: The door was unlocked.

Elaine: Jeffrey had to cancel your appointment.

Robert: Oh.

Elaine: He said he couldn't get back till six-thirty or so.

Robert: Oh, well . . .

Feel free to wait.

Robert: No. I—

Elaine: Have him. Robert. Please. Take him. It will help my suit if you're both more open about it . . . If you can convert him into something . . . human. I mean it, seriously.

Robert: I think I'd better—

Elaine *(overlapping)*: No, please, you do owe me. This.

(Short pause)

Elaine: The . . . absurdly, the insane thing is I like you. That's—Not only do I have nothing against you, in another universe, in another time, dimension, I would want to be your friend. I think you're . . . incredibly sweet. I see what draws him in . . . Attracts him.

Act II

Robert: I guess you two have had . . .

Elaine: I'm not deaf, dumb and blind, all evidence . . . Is there anything you want to say to me? (*Short pause*) Nothing?

Robert: I'm sorry.

(*Pause*)

Elaine: Robert? May I . . . ? What is unconditional love like? Where . . . Can you tell me? How do you . . . Where do you find it? In yourself. To give. Much less get. I'm not even thinking about that . . . that would be . . . too terrible to contemplate. (*Pause*) I'm asking. It's a real question.

Robert: This is . . . I'm sorry, this is weird.

Elaine: This? No, this is nothing. The higher you get in these hills, the weirder it gets. Sit. (*Pause*) Please.

(*Robert sits*)

Elaine: Salad?

(*Pause. She places the plastic container and bottled water in her carry-all*)

Elaine: You and Malcolm . . . where did you find it in yourself . . . How did you manage to put up with all the . . . *literally* the shit? So much . . .

(*Pause*)

Elaine: How? . . . Please. (*Pause*) So much . . . oh . . . compromise . . .

Robert: I never lied to him or accepted one. (*Pause*) That's what made it possible. We simply said: no more lies.

(*Pause*)

Elaine: No lies. (*Pause*) Coming from you . . . you have to admit . . . it's, well it's—

Robert: I know.

Elaine: *Ohhh*, no more lies, what a good idea, why didn't I think of it? . . . It's funny.

Robert: I never lied to you.

(*Pause*)

Elaine: And what is it you think I lied about?

Robert: I wasn't referring—

Elaine: I know Jeffrey likes men.

Robert: I should go.

Elaine: Wait. Please. What is it you think I lied about?

(*Pause*)

Robert: I didn't say you lied.

Elaine: But what do you think? (*Pause*) I'm asking for your opinion.

(*Pause*)

Robert: I don't know enough . . .

(*Pause*)

Elaine: If you had to venture a guess, you would say I . . . failed to see, I did . . . what? (*Pause*) From your perspective. That's all. (*Pause*) Help me.

(*Pause*)

Robert: I would say . . . No, I can't—

Elaine (*overlapping*): Yes, you can.

(*Pause*)

Robert: I would say that . . . I would say that . . . (*Short pause*) Your anger . . . at what . . . the things that have happened . . . All the things. In your whole life. Should be . . . filtered through . . . You are responsible. For all of it. Everything. You.

(*Pause*)

Elaine: Excu—?

Robert: Are responsible for everything. All the things that happen to us, that make us feel like a victim, it's   It's all a lesson. Look within.

Elaine: Oh.

Robert: Find what is positive.

Elaine: Well. (*Pause*) I will . . . I'll look for the positive in, yes, the lesson in losing Jeff. In having you fuck him behind my back—

(*Pause*)

Robert: I guess . . .

Elaine: Repeatedly. Surreptitiously, and all the while I'm trying to be generous—

Robert (*overlapping*): I should really—

Elaine: NO! You will not walk out of here. (*Pause*) . . . trying to be generous. To you.

(*Pause*)

Robert: You shouldn't . . . You shouldn't do me any favors. Really. Self-salvation is for any man the immediate task.

(*Pause*)

Elaine: Self-salvation is for any man . . . the immediate task.

(*Pause*)

Robert: Please tell Jeffrey I came by.

(*He turns to leave*)

Elaine: Arckangell is dead. Robert.

(*Robert stops*)

Elaine: He died. He had to be deleted from his hard drive. (*Short pause*) He doesn't even have a floppy anymore, he doesn't have anything. No corporeal being. No spirit. (*Silence*) Self-salvation for all of us, thank you.

Robert: You . . .

Elaine: Yes.

Robert: You bribed Foss. Or . . .

Elaine: The nice thing . . .

Robert: You robbed him.

Elaine: . . . is . . . that you will never know. Professional thieves, unlike screenwriters, have no ego, they feel no need to leave their names emblazoned all over their work. (*Short pause*) Tell Jeff when you see him that this is the bare minimum of what—Never mind.

(*Elaine writes a note and places it on the table*)

Elaine: Excuse me, I have to finish packing.

(*She exits*)

Robert: Malcolm? . . . Baby . . . ? Please . . . Oh . . . Oh . . . Malcolm.

(*Robert's eyes dart among the plants; he yanks up one by the roots, uses his pen knife to shave bits of the root into his hand, pops them in his mouth. He chews for a moment, then spits them out, wiping his tongue on the back of his shirt*)

Robert: No . . . (*He takes a swig of bottled water from Elaine's carry-all, then spits it out*) No.

(*Again. He stares into the bag. Pause. He looks at Elaine's note*)

Robert: Malcolm? . . .

(*Silence. Robert shaves off more of the root, turns to face the house before removing the salad container and lifting the lid, dropping in the bits. He is replacing the lid when Elaine re-emerges with a suitcase. Robert returns the salad to the bag and drops the plant out of sight*)

Robert: He wouldn't kill you. It was a joke.

Elaine: The humor of which—Tell him the story of how you asked me if he would really go through with it, he'll—

Robert: He wouldn't.

Elaine: —enjoy it.

Robert: Do you need any help? Packing?

Elaine: You really do have a problem with anger, don't you?

(*She spots one last item she wishes to take; as she retrieves it, Robert lifts the travel bag and brings it to her*)

Elaine: You know how to lock up?

Robert: I should go.

Elaine: Yes.

Robert: I'm sorry.

(*Pause*)

Elaine: Yes.

(*Pause*)

———————

(*Robert's apartment. Robert alone*)

Robert: I gave it all, everything over to god . . . gave everything up . . . She would or she wouldn't eat it. Either way . . . I gave it . . . then threw up for over an hour, nothing coming up but air . . . offering it . . . The knife I threw off the San Diego Freeway . . . offering it, too . . . My fingerprints were on everything, but then they would be . . . I offered them . . . Her note in its entirety reads: "This is nowhere near what you deserve." Having written enough of them in my mind, I know what a suicide note should sound like. I offered them all, all of them up to god . . .

(*Pause*)

Robert: There was no Malcolm, none I could see. To lose him again . . . Maybe he was there, beside me screaming: NO! Stop!, don't, life, every breath of it is precious, you mustn't kill so much as an *ant* . . . NO! ROBERT!

(*Pause*)

Robert: Maybe.

(*Loud knocking*)

Robert: But I couldn't hear.

Jeffrey: ROBERT! OPEN UP, I NEED TO TALK TO YOU. ROBERT! (*More pounding. Robert lets Jeffrey in*) What did you do? What did you say to her?

Robert: Elaine?

Jeffrey: What did you show her?

Robert: Nothing.

Jeffrey: I don't believe you.

Robert: I'm sorry about that.

Jeffrey: What did you do? TELL ME!

Robert: I just went over there for our meeting and she was all riled up . . .

Jeffrey: Oh, yes, you did nothing, you said nothing.

Robert: No.

Jeffrey: Nothing to her at all.

Robert: No, I'm sorry, I—

Jeffrey: *YOU* are sorry? Do I seem enshrouded in illusion to you, Robert? I'm—Do I seem less real to you? If I'm making sure my children and wife and I and our grandchildren all of us never have to subjugate ourselves to anyone, can live anywhere, and once in a while I get to make a movie I like—I'm sorry I don't live up to your standards, trouble is I'm bisexual; I like both. You want the truth, but—You're lucky to be all one thing. I'm not. I'm not hiding in my marriage, I need my marriage . . . and not just for business reasons, Jesus Christ, half of Hollywood is out of the fucking closet, they're all on the cover of magazines, proclaiming their pride, it's not the old days . . . Were you so . . . ? I'm sorry I've corrupted your poor little . . . Give back the million if it makes you so unhappy you have to . . . piss in other peoples' wells.

(*Pause*)

Robert: I . . . did not say anything to Elaine. She was very freaked out . . . She was packing . . .

Jeffrey: Yes, I got the note. I'm using your phone.

(*Jeffrey dials*)

Robert: She said she figured it out. I said I was very very sorry.

Jeffrey: You have no reason to tell me the truth.

(*Jeffrey hangs up*)

Robert: I have no reason to lie. (*Pause*) If she told you I said something—

Jeffrey: She said you faxed her something.

Robert: That would be . . . I don't have a fax machine. Remember?

(*Pause. Jeffrey dials again*)

Jeffrey: Liz? Any . . . ? What? No, tell me . . . Tell me now . . . No. No. No. No . . . God . . . Oh . . . Liz . . . Noooooo. No. Please . . . Say . . . *Oh! No!* . . . It can't . . . Say this is not . . . true . . .

Robert: "We learn from our suffering to reduce and finally eliminate its cause." They died . . . senselessly . . . his children, the woman he loved . . . slammed into a concrete divider at seventy miles an hour . . . dead for no reason . . . Reaching out to stop it, nothing he or anyone could do . . . Maybe now someone understands. No one to take the blame for these terrible deaths . . . Dead for no reason . . . And this time I'm god.

Jeffrey: Help me. All of them.

(*Robert comforts him*)

Robert: I know . . .

Jeffrey: She drove them into a wall. How could she . . . Oh . . . Oh . . .

Robert: "No one owns the life that flows through them . . . any more than the electric light bulb owns the electricity that flows through it . . ." (*Pause*) No one.

(*Robert alone*)

Robert: They wouldn't even look for the poison in her bloodstream. Perhaps it wasn't even there. Perhaps she just lost control of the vehicle. Or turned the wheel . . . Perhaps there was a bee in the car . . . Who knows? (*Pause*) We have no control.

(*Pause*)

Robert: The movie of course did not do well. Because I hadn't stuck to my guns, my instincts, and followed my own course . . . But each thing, no matter what it is, is a learning—it's an opportunity: to learn the rules. To perform. And I would do well. I will. There are no limits to what I can accomplish.

(*Pause*)

Robert: "All men contain the potentiality of Enlightenment, and the process therefore consists in becoming what you are."

(*Pause*)

Robert: Done.